Carving
Humorous Santas

Paul F. & Camille J. Bolinger
Photography by Pat McChesney

4880 Lower Valley Rd. Atglen, PA 19310 USA

Dedication

My thanks to Camille, my wife and partner, for all the years of help, support, and guidance. Also our love to our son Jake Bear Bolinger, who keeps on smiling amid the daily grind of growing up in a woodcarver's studio.

Acknowledgments

Pat McChesney is a wizard of many things including photography. There is no way to properly thank Pat for dropping everything else in his busy family and work life and running here with camera in hand. Thanks Pat.

Java Jumpstart's bony little legs, latte, and that "can't quite wake up" look on his face are a hit. This figure is approximately 7 1/2" tall.

Back view of Java Jumpstart.

Published by Schiffer Publishing Ltd.
4880 Lower Valley Road
Atglen, PA 19310
Phone: (610) 593-1777; Fax: (610) 593-2002
E-mail: schifferbk@aol.com
Please write for a free catalog.
This book may be purchased from the publisher.
Please include $3.95 for shipping.
Try your bookstore first.

We are interested in hearing from authors with book ideas on related subjects.

Foreword

Kurt S. Adler, Inc. recently celebrated its 50th anniversary designing, manufacturing, and selling Christmas themed items. In those 50 years, our company has seen the coming and going of fads and trends but Santa has always remained a large part of our business. Santa has come in so many images it is sometimes difficult to believe that one figure could have so many incarnations. Even now, in 1997, when the thousands of products we offer range from trees, to lights, to collector glass ornaments, Santa is more popular than ever and is still appearing in many different looks.

The humorous Santas designed and carved by Paul Bolinger are a fun part of our offering. From his most popular figure "Will Work for Cookies" to "Christmas is Like a Box of Chocolates" and even "Christmas Shopping — Been There Done That", Paul has found a way to bring Santa down from the North Pole and into everyday situations. These pieces bring a humor to the world of Santa that many find irresistible and show that Santa is just one of us.

Howard Adler
New York

Contents

Introduction

One of the things I create, as a professional woodcarver, is a line of collectible humorous Santas named "The Ho, Ho, Ho Gang." These Santas are reproduced from the original woodcarvings in cast resin by Kurt S. Adler, Inc. of New York and sold around U.S. and Canada. Designing this line has given me a great outlet for my creative energy and also has been a great learning experience. In this book I will share some of what I have learned with you.

In the past four years I have crossed and re-crossed the U.S. visiting our customers and doing personal appearances in stores that sell our Santas. In those four years I have met many wonderful customers and lots of friendly woodcarvers too. In visiting with customers and fellow carvers alike, one of the most frequently asked questions concerns how I keep coming up with new ideas for Santas. In this book I hope to help you understand the process I use to formulate a design and bring it into being.

When I first started carving years ago, I struggled for ideas about what I wanted to carve and I hungered for inspiration. Some of the most helpful books I found were not "how-to" books but were instead "idea books;" by that I mean they were books crammed with drawings or pictures of things that other people had carved. One in particular, I remember, was touted as containing thousands of ideas and it did. I used that book and the others to find practice pieces and to let my mind wander.

Inspiration is a funny thing; it can come from almost anywhere. Let me assure you that, as the saying goes, there is nothing new under the sun. Many times I have come up with what I think is a dynamite first-time topic only to find out somehow that it has already been done by someone else. I don't let that stop me if the idea is a good one. Don't be overly concerned with the possibility that your design is copying someone else's. If you are not consciously copying then go ahead and work out your design; it will be different.

For example, I can't tell you how many Santas I have seen riding on animals and fish. It's probably a good thing that Santa wasn't around in the time of Noah or he might have tried to ride all the livestock aboard the ark. I've seen Santa on a bear, a polar bear, a horse, an elk, a moose, a camel, an elephant, a tiger, a rooster, a goose, a swan, a pig, a trout, and probably others too. I have done Santa on a turtle and on a rabbit myself and will still be doing Santa on a bear sometime. Why? Because I don't think that the first time someone did Santa riding on something was the last time anyone else could use that concept. Think of how many different Santas on bears there could be and how yours would be different.

It is my sincere hope that this book will serve as an idea book for today's woodcarvers and will motivate you to look around and find other inspiration for your work too. I have included patterns for you but also an extensive gallery that shows many humorous Santas in different forms and sizes that should provide you hours of daydreaming as you let your mind wander in the design process.

Enjoy yourself and have fun carving but also please remember that all the Santas shown here are copyrighted and cannot be reproduced for commercial purposes. Enjoy them as inspirations.

If you are interested in any one of these figures as a study cast, many of them are available. You can usually find them at a shop not far from where you live. If you cannot find them on the market, you may send me a SASE for the price list and availability at 4405 S. Echo Ct., Spokane, WA 99223.

Chapter One
Where Did He Get That Idea?

I'm a looker, a listener, and a daydreamer. Don't get me wrong; anybody that knows me will tell you I am very outgoing. I do my share of joke telling and general visiting, but I do make a focused effort to look, listen, and also to daydream. How are these habits employed in the design process?

Go shopping! I love to shop. I don't mean at the department store or the grocery store; I mean at those quaint little shops where you find the little doo-dads and gee-gaws of life — places where you can find inspiration. Go where there is something unique to look at. Looking is the first part of the design process for me. I need to cram as many images into my brain as I can and store them there for future recall.

Find good books. I love to read books with lots of pictures. Books by artists that I could never match for style, detail, or appeal intrigue me. Books with lots of little drawings or pictures are a visual feast. Books by artists show me how other people see the world, process it, and then recreate it in their own way.

Buy good magazines. I like to look at magazines. Notice I said "look at" magazines and not "read" magazines. Occasionally I do read magazines but mostly I just look at the pictures. Decorating magazines are my favorite. With page upon page of rooms full of the things people have collected and displayed, these magazines are one of the richest sources of inspiration.

Show people your work and listen to what they say. Listening is critical. I have more than the usual opportunity to listen since I spend many days a year out in stores with customers actually looking at my work and other people's work. Helping a customer find something to purchase is a very intense learning experience. You can imagine looking, then discussing, then looking again, then looking at something else, and finally going back to the first item. I have actually had customers take as long as an hour to make a selection but that is a rare customer indeed.

Listening involves hearing not only what someone likes about a certain item but also what they don't like about that item. Learning what people don't like is critical but it can also be painful if you take it personally. I learned years ago, when I was showing my work at art & wine festivals and street fairs, that people are insensitive and can be very rude. It's a pretty humbling experience to have someone stand in front of your work and knock it. It is still amazing to me that there are people in the world who feel compelled to tell you that they don't like what you made instead of just quietly turning and going on with their own business. Thank goodness those types are not prevalent.

Even today, I still have listening experiences that help me keep my feet firmly on the ground. Since many of my personal appearances are in stores, I find myself among displays of many different items only some of which are mine. It is a learning experience to be visiting with a customer who then passes right over my work and selects something from a nearby display for me to sign that is not from my collection. The customer, of course, feels badly about it but I have learned to focus on what it was about the item that made them select it. Maybe I will get an idea from that experience for one of next year's new pieces.

Experiences like that have made me a detached listener. I am genuinely interested in learning what the customer has to say about the item and I know they are not saying it about me — they are teaching me.

Listening also means being aware of what is going on in the world and, in particular, what is funny. Bringing Santa into our world means that I must know what is going in our world. I try to be aware of "pop culture," which is difficult since I don't watch much TV. I do listen to a lot of news-talk radio, so I know generally what is on people's minds and what things are topical. It does take judgment to decide right now what will still be topical or funny a year later when the products I design hit the market.

Daydreaming is a key element of the design process. You can substitute the words "thinking about" for daydreaming if that word gives you a negative feeling. I am very positive about daydreaming and the beneficial effect it has on the design process. Daydreaming, to me, is simply relaxing with eyes open or closed, and letting your mind run wild in a more or less controlled direction. I try to find time each day to daydream about designs I want to do and I always use the moments just before going to sleep at night to focus on my design work.

Daydreaming leads to the generation and refinement of ideas. Going over all those things you have observed and heard and letting them stew in your daydreams will lead to designs or at least the beginnings of designs. I tend to keep a pad of paper and a pencil with me when I relax to daydream. That way I can record any good ideas that come to mind so that I can later recall them and work on their refinement. Daydreaming for me is a kind of mental drawing process wherein I visualize the design I need and then work on it in the most easily modifiable of all mediums — my imagination.

Without sounding too far out, let me tell you a story about daydreaming, otherwise known as visualization. Years ago, long before I took up carving, I worked in a windowless office in a windowless building on a top secret government project. At night I was studying for an MBA degree. One of our professors walked us through a visualization exercise where we were to relax completely and then let our mind wander to a point years in the future and try to visualize what were our surroundings. I remember vividly seeing, in my mind, that I was seated working on something with my hands and to my left was a window through which I could see many beautiful green trees. I thought I was typing something, perhaps a book and I also thought that maybe I was just doing some wishful thinking about having a window at work. Years later I was at work in my carving studio, using my hands, and looking out the window at all the beautiful green trees outside my cabin when it hit me. Here I was — just like I had "dreamed" about in that night class years before!

I'm not trying to say that the one incident lead to the other. I would, however, venture the idea that subconsciously I longed for such an environment and pastime and that on a subconscious level I must have worked to fulfill that longing. One day it came true.

There is power in the subconscious and daydreaming is a great relaxing way to use that power.

"On Strike for More Cookies" — this fellow was so hungry he couldn't wait to get home so he started eating his sign. This figure is approximately 8 1/2" tall.

Back view.

6

Chapter Two
The Elements of Design

What Do People See?

What people actually see varies widely but there are some generalities I have observed. Before going into the details, let me tell you a story that will illustrate what differences there are in people's observations. Once I was doing a carving demonstration at a store where my things were being sold. I had a Santa I was finishing that must have looked complete to one customer since she wanted that Santa very much - at least until I pointed out to her that I hadn't yet carved and added his hands. She actually hadn't seen something as important as that. This story illustrates that some people, most I believe, tend to see in generalities. There are a few keen observers but most people tend to generalize.

For the purposes of this book I have grouped the elements of design into these six topics: subject, color, size/shape, movement/action, detail, and texture. These elements are listed in their order of importance to me.

The subject of the design is the thing you are trying to make. In a humorous Santa it must also have a surprise, a twist, or a hook. It must have something that makes it amusing or humorous. This can be supplied by what the figure is doing, what the figure is saying, or how the figure is posed. One early example of a humorous pose showed a fat Santa struggling to get into or out of a chimney. It was titled "Will He Make It?" People liked the look but when they heard or read the title and put it together with the look they were hooked. I find in many of my designs that the twist is in the writing; almost a play on words using a visual image. In many of my designs you can see that I have actually put the writing onto the piece so that the viewer will see it along with the piece. A great example of the power of the message is "Christmas Shopping - Been There Done That" which is really just a cute Santa with a banner in each hand. Even though he is cute, the reason he sells is the written message.

"Christmas Shopping - Been There Done That." Approximately 7".

People tend to see color first. It seems that brighter is better too — up to a point. I have not seen any successful "International Orange Glow in The Dark" Santas. The colors for Santa need to be appropriate; by that I mean that there are traditional colors for Santa. Don't worry though, historically Santa has had a good range of pleasing colors and a little research will show you these.

While Santa does have a traditional color scheme, it is a fact that colors go in and out of style. Today's and tomorrow's colors are the ones to use if you can. The colors we are using for 1998 include very bright reds, as shown on the piece "Will Work for Cookies."

"Will Work for Cookies." Approximately 7".

In this chapter I will show you a few of my designs and review for you the origin of the idea, the development of the idea, and how the elements of design are represented in the piece. The first example to be analyzed is the figure "Will Work for Cookies." The figure shown here front and back is actually a second version of the original design. The original design was in production three years and was my best seller even though the price was somewhat high (from $35 - $45 retail). Because of its popularity, this design is a good example for study.

"Will Work for Cookies." Approximately 7".

It is probably not the first thing you think about as a woodcarver but color is critical. My wife paints my carvings and does a great job but we do discuss colors before and during the painting process. It is not unusual to have a piece repainted after it is considered ready; even minor changes in color can make a big difference.

Color also can imply richness and depth. A single color can be "flat" and unappealing whereas a plaid or pattern can add depth and richness. Clothing, Christmas decorations, Christmas stockings, Christmas cards, and the like can be a good source of color and texture inspiration.

I am not an expert in color and have a special struggle with color combinations. There are books, charts, and devices that can help you work out color combinations but still the best way to learn is to look around. See what works for other pieces. See what color combinations are pleasant to you and to others.

Size is another critical design element. Items can be designed for a specific purpose such as a tree ornament. Obviously, a tree ornament must have size and weight limits or it will not be useful. Most of my pieces are in the category of item referred to as "table pieces." Generally for these smaller is better since people tend not to have a lot of space for display. Of course, the size must be consistent with the overall idea. In the case of "Boxers or Briefs" I made Santa coming out of a small box so there would be lots of room to have his outstretched arms and the underwear too.

Details can be eye catching even though they often are not part of the subject or message. In my new design for a fishing Santa, there are details everywhere and these do relate to the subject. Look at all the various types of bait Santa has and also the detailing in his coat; these items all add visual interest.

Action or movement is also an important element of design. Santa doing something is more appealing that Santa just sitting there doing nothing. It isn't necessary for Santa to be doing handstands but a little hint of movement or action will help the design. Many of my early pieces concentrated on the "story line" and didn't contain the necessary element of movement or action. Take a look at "Surprise" in the photo gallery to see what I mean and compare that to "Boxers or Briefs" which shows action. While these pieces were successful, they would have represented better design if they had contained this element.

"Boxers or Briefs." Approximately 6 1/2".

Chapter Three
Some Designs Analyzed

The idea for this design originated out of the public concern over homeless people. While there certainly are a number of homeless people with real problems, there are also many examples of the other kind. Everyone by now has had experienced first hand, or at least has heard, of someone stopping to offer work to a person with a "will work" sign. The outcome of such encounters usually involves the homeless "worker" refusing the job. These encounters have made the "will work" sign a pop culture icon. Once I had decided to ask myself the question "what would Santa work for" the idea was born and the design process started.

There were two questions that had to be answered for this design. The first question was "what would Santa actually work for"? Did he want cookies and milk? Did he want to be kissing Momma underneath the mistletoe? Did he want a day off? Did he want a new sleigh?

The second question that had to be answered was "what kind of work would he do?" Would he wash windows? How about shovel snow? Would he deliver packages? In the first version of this design, I decided to answer the first question but leave the second question unanswered.

The hook or twist on the first design is a poorly lettered sign, like one done by a homeless person, hanging from Santa's hand that reads simply "Will Work for Cookies" and a look on Santa's face that indicates he is downcast. I went with the most basic version and put cookies and milk into the figure. Hence, this Santa has a tray with cookies, milk, and a chocolate eclair in his hand. I love chocolate eclairs so the chocolate eclair represents what I "will work for."

"Fishing Santa." Approximately 8".

In the remake of this design, shown here, I was attempting to reduce the price to capitalize on the popularity of the design and also to improve the design if I could. Time will tell whether everything works, but in the design process I tried to: improve the hook or twist by answering the question about what kind of work he would do, improve the color scheme by making it brighter, improve the overall look by adding details in bold color to catch the shopper's eye, change the sign from a simple cardboard sign to a more whimsical sign written on a chocolate chip cookie, and last but not least to add a little touch of movement by having it look as if Santa is thrusting the sign up into the air to get some attention.

One of my classic older designs is "Bald is Beautiful." This design represents a great example of re-thinking a piece. The first idea for this design came from a friend of mine who is bald and is always telling stories about his bald head. Listening to him I decided that if he was having so much fun being bald then Santa could too. Originally this Santa had a removable hat that sat down over his bald head but would also hang from his hand. The title was intended to be "Hat's Off to You" and the idea was that you could remove the hat and be surprised by his bald head. That design was rejected, and rightly so. I liked this bald Santa so much I didn't want to give up, so I came up with a way to modify the design.

"Bald is Beautiful." Approximately 10".

One night watching TV I realized that most everyone in the country was aware of the name Rogaine since commercials were appearing almost constantly. I decided that Santa could have a giant sized tube of "hair gain," a name intended to recall the sound of Rogaine, and a giant-sized comb to emphasize that he was working on his giant-sized hair loss problem. He also needed something to show what the overall hook was, so I devised a nice heart shaped sign that said "bald is beautiful." My wife later modified that to "bald sure is beautiful" since that balanced better on the layout of the sign.

The color on this piece was muted so that the bald head would not become invisible. The rest of the piece was kept simple so that the main design elements, the hair gain and the comb, would stand out. The piece does not have any movement or action and probably would be better if it did. Overall the design was simple but it worked.

The last example to be analyzed is "Behave-o-Meter." The idea for this design came to me when I was listening to Christmas carols. As one song says, "he knows if you've been bad or good, so be good for goodness' sake." I was sure most everyone would remember that Santa will bring you a present if you are good but he will bring you a lump of coal or a switch if you aren't so good. I went to work putting all these ideas into one design. In daydreaming about how to show Santa "knowing" something, I remembered that I always liked to watch the "applause-o-meters" on those old TV shows. Then I knew that Santa must surely have a "behave-o-meter" to help him decide who gets what for Christmas.

I pulled together all the elements of my thought process into the design. Santa is standing on his "behave-o-meter" which has a needle that can move back and forth from bad to good. On the top of the "behave-o-meter" it says "he knows." In one hand he has a lump of coal clearly marked; I discarded the idea of having Santa hold some switches since they would have been too small, too confusing, and too breakable. In the other hand he has a present in gold wrapping. Everything is said right there.

The colors aren't particularly bright in this piece but they are appropriate. Santa is mostly beard so that your eye tends to focus on the "behave-o-meter" instead of Santa; that's good. There is some movement shown by Santa raising up the two possible gift outcomes. There is texture in Santa's beard and overall depth in the piece because of the different items shown. There is also something else in the design called "play value" since the needle does move and you can set it to wherever you wish. Perhaps your spouse is acting up a little, then you can react by moving the needle from good to bad and hope that he or she gets the message.

"Behave-o-Meter." Approximately 7".

Chapter Four
Carving and Painting
the "Chocoholic" Santa

The tools I use for this project are standard carver's tools, chisels, gouges, and a knife. I use a urethane covered mallet to keep the sound down and to cushion the damage to my tool handles. I generally mail order my tools by the shape needed and try not to spend too much on tools.

Although I used these tools for the project, there is no reason you can't make it with just a set of knives if you wish. All the cuts I show would still work with knives and actually some of them would be faster; particularly ones like the "stop cuts."

For beginners my big caution is, "do not try to remove too much at one time." As you will see, this is a process of "peeling the onion" and moving around and around the object to keep everything in balance. Taking too much at one time can lead to distortions and other balance problems. Take your time and take it slow — you may go over the same area three or four times before you have it down to final size.

Be prepared to draw the pattern on the piece over and over again. I always keep reference to the centerline of the piece and then draw details onto it. The details are carved away and then redrawn over and over again.

In this project, as in others, I sometimes stray a little from the pattern but that can lead to improvements. In this case I decided at the last minute not to carve Santa's hand at the end of his outstretched arm but to add a hand onto the arm. Also Santa's hat and hair line came out slightly different on the final piece but I'm not sure you would notice that in the photos. Note that the heart was made and added to the carving — this was planned.

Enlarge 115% for original size.

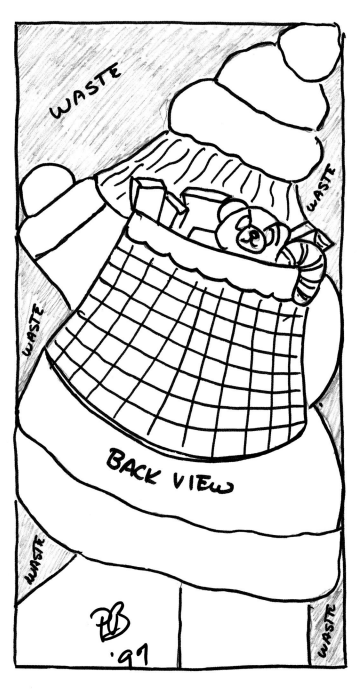

"CHOCOHOLIC" SANTA 4"x4" BASSWOOD

CARVE OR PAINT YOUR OWN DETAILS

PUT YOUR OWN PATTERN ON HIS SACK

WASTE

BACK VIEW

'97

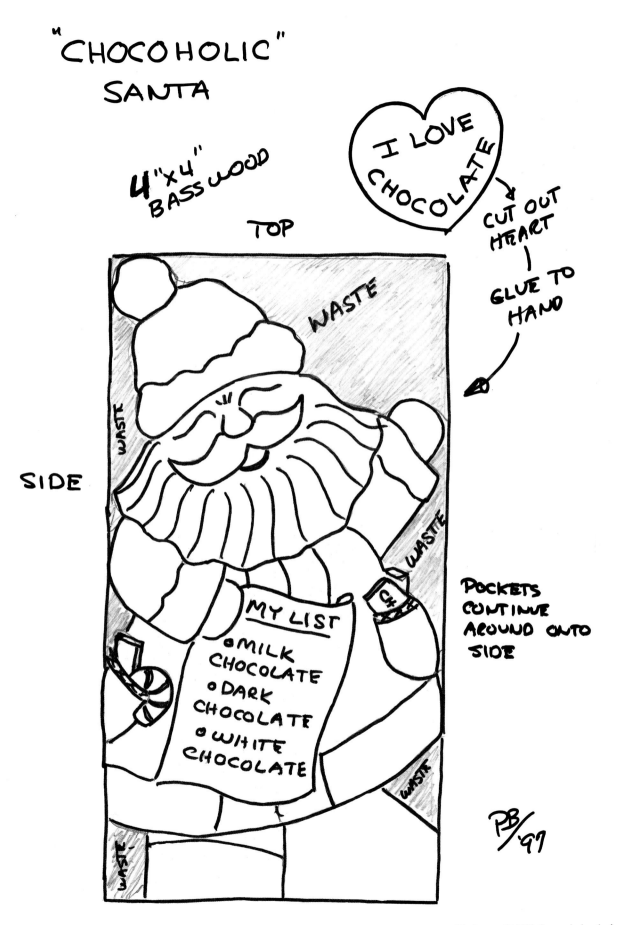

"CHOCOHOLIC" SANTA

4"x4" BASSWOOD

I LOVE CHOCOLATE

CUT OUT HEART

GLUE TO HAND

TOP

WASTE

SIDE

WASTE

WASTE

MY LIST
o MILK CHOCOLATE
o DARK CHOCOLATE
o WHITE CHOCOLATE

POCKETS CONTINUE AROUND ONTO SIDE

WASTE

WASTE

PB/97

Enlarge 115% for original size.

This is the back view of the completed Santa. Note the location and size of details.

This is the right side view of the completed Santa.

This is the front view of the finished "chocoholic" Santa. Look closely at the figure and try to set the details into your mind's eye. This will help you as you carve the piece. This finished Santa is approximately 8" tall.

This is the left side view of the completed Santa.

Here is a close-up of the woodcarver's arm I use to hold the work. The arm is made of oak and clamped to the workbench. You can see some of my tools on the bench. I don't have a large selection, just enough to do the job.

Back view of 4" X 4" basswood block with pattern transferred.

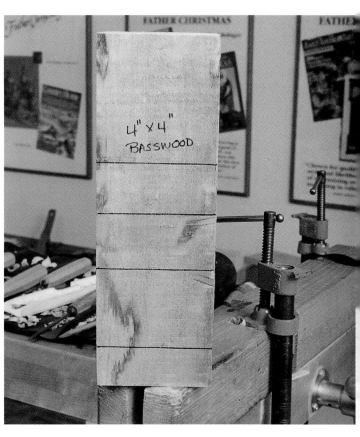

Front view of the 4" X 4" basswood block with the pattern transferred onto the block. I used carbon paper to trace the pattern onto the block and then I darkened it greatly so that it would show in the photo.

The side view of the block shows the lines drawn to connect the front and back patterns. These lines will serve as guides for the cuts made with a hand saw. I don't own a band saw so I use a hand saw and my gouges to rough out the piece. If you own or have access to a band saw, you may wish to use that to rough the block out.

I used a crosscut hand saw to saw into the sides of the block where the lines indicated. Depth of cut was determined by watching the saw blade on the front and back patterns.

With the block secured tightly to the carver's arm, I use a large shallow gouge to remove the waste wood. At the top you can split the block along the grain all the way down to the saw kerf (or saw cut).

This view shows the woodcarver's screw inserted into the bottom of the block. The screw handle is in place and I have added a large washer that helps protect the oak arm from being too easily crushed by the screw handle.

Use a large gouge to cut down from the top to the saw kerf and remove waste.

19

Use a large gouge to cut up to the saw kerf.

Use gouges to remove the waste from the other cuts.

This view shows the waste removed from above and below the one saw cut.

Remove waste from the saw cuts on the opposite side of the block too.

View of the front of the piece showing the waste removed from both sides. This block is now roughed out and ready for carving.

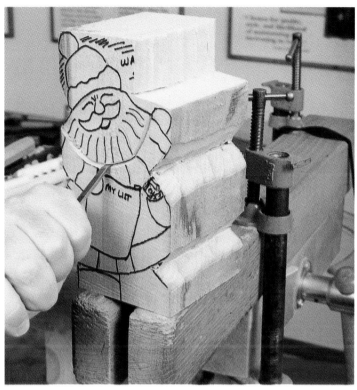

Use a firmer (a.k.a. a straight chisel) to put a "stop cut" into the block in the groove under Santa's beard.

Use a "V" gouge to cut a groove along the bottom of Santa's beard.

Use a large gouge to begin removing wood from under the beard. Run your gouge up to the stop cut you just made under the beard. Remove the wood to a depth of 1/4" - 3/8".

Remove the wood all along the stop cut.

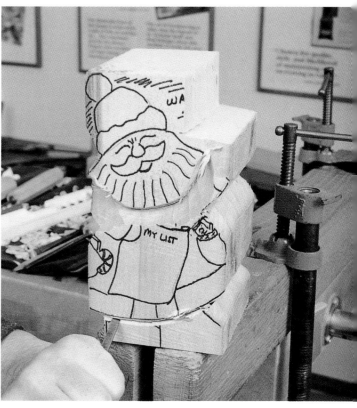

Use a firmer to make a stop cut in the groove.

Use the "V" gouge to make a groove along the bottom of Santa's coat.

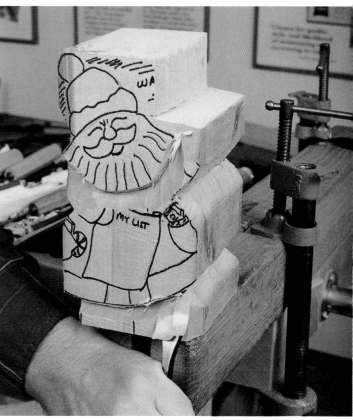

Remove the wood up to the stop cut to a depth of 1/4" - 3/8" using a large gouge.

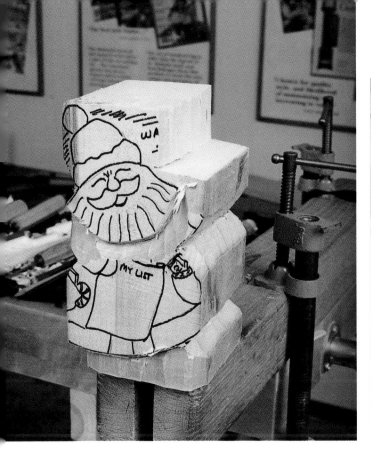

Front view of the piece at this point.

Use a small "U" gouge to make a semi-circular stop cut around Santa's mitten.

Use a "V" gouge to outline around Santa's list.

Use a medium "U" gouge to remove the wood below the mitten and on the arm. Go slightly around the bottom of the beard and slightly onto the left side.

23

Use a medium "U" gouge to cut in along the top of Santa's list.

Use a large gouge to begin sloping Santa's hat toward the back. Slope it back 1" to 1 1/2". Note: During this process I uncovered a hidden blemish on Santa but I continued to carve.

Use a large gouge to remove the remaining waste around the side of Santa's hat.

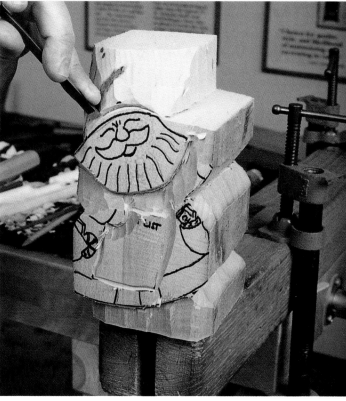

Use a small "V" gouge to cut a groove along the hat line at the top of Santa's face, then set in a stop cut using a firmer.

Use a medium shallow "U" gouge to remove the wood from Santa's forehead cutting up under his hat.

Work on pushing Santa's arm back from his beard.

Use a large gouge to slope the hat back farther now.

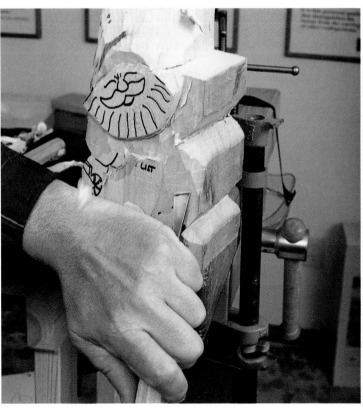

Use a large gouge to begin rounding Santa's coat under his arm and onto his side.

Roughly mark off the backward facing edge of Santa's upraised left arm and draw a sloping line to mark his coat from under the arm to the pattern on the back.

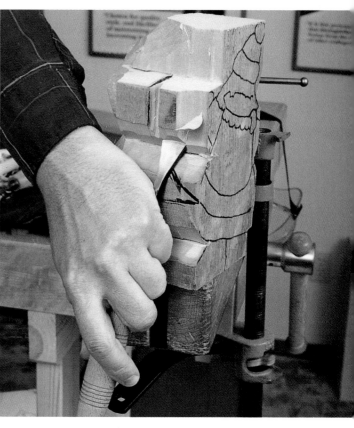

Use a large gouge to remove the waste from behind Santa's arm.

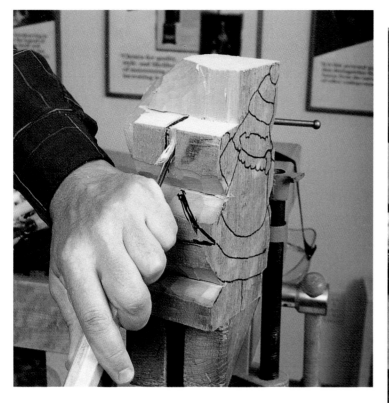

Use a "V" gouge to cut a vertical groove along the back of Santa's arm.

Remove the waste from the side of the hat and slope the hat along the pattern line.

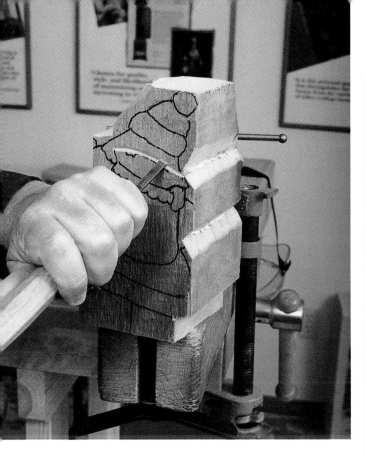

Cut a groove along the line above the top of Santa's bag. Make a stop cut there.

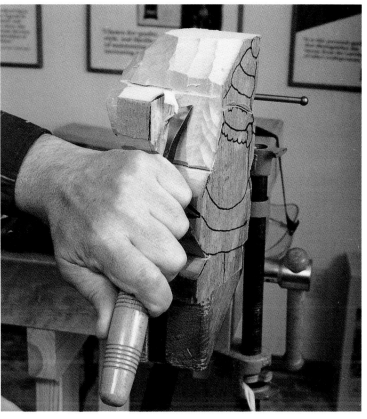

Cut away the remaining waste in the area as shown.

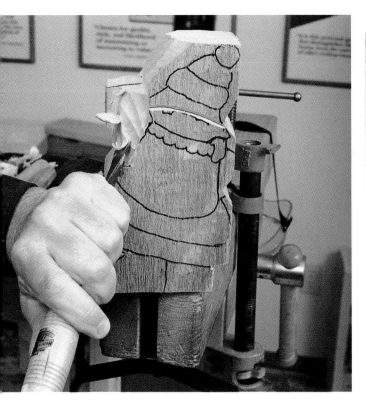

Cut away the waste at the side of the bag.

Make a groove and stop cut at the bottom of the back of Santa's bag.

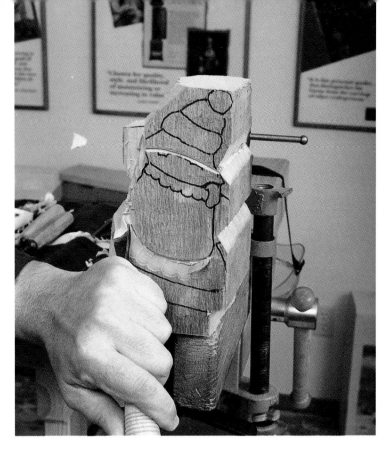

Remove the wood below the bottom of the bag to a depth of 1/4" - 3/8".

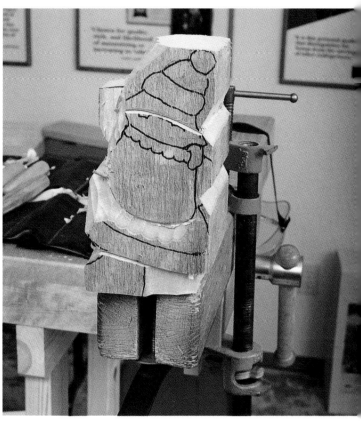

Remove the wood from under the bottom of the coat. Don't go very deep at this time.

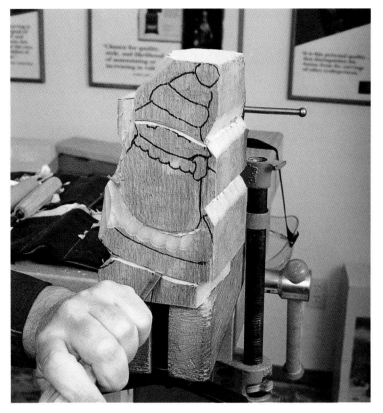

Make a groove and stop cut at the bottom of the back of Santa's coat.

Slope the hat farther back on the other side.

Put a stop cut along the bottom of the hat.

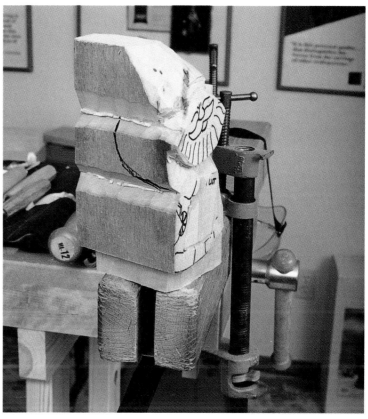

Mark the bottom of Santa's right arm. Use your eye to tell you what looks good.

Remove the wood up to the bottom of the hat.

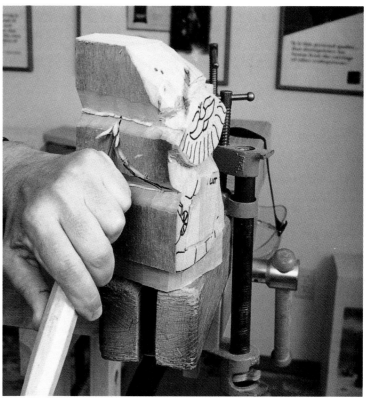

Use a "V" gouge to outline the coat sleeve.

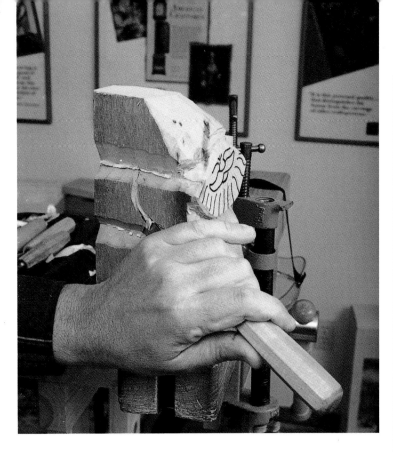

Use a medium "U" gouge to remove the wood under the arm.

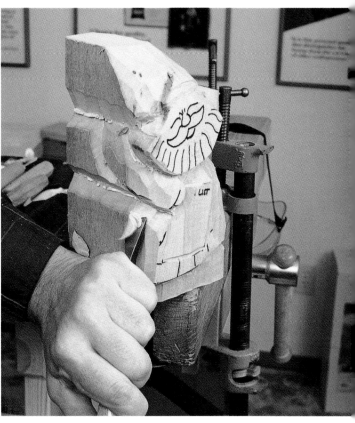

Round the coat from the front to the side.

Remove the wood and give the arm some shape.

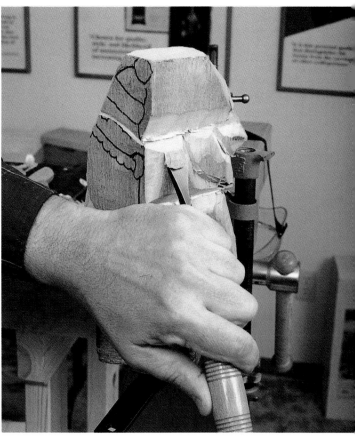

Remove excess wood from behind the arm.

Cut down to the stop cut you made earlier above the bag.

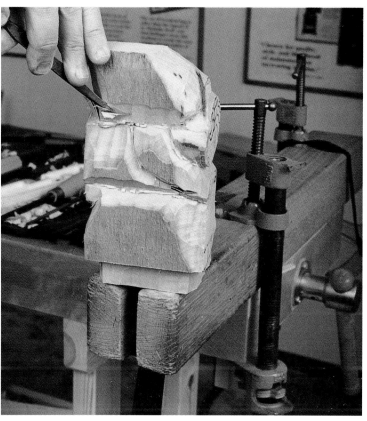

Shape down the back and side of the hat.

Remove excess wood above the line. This is where Santa's hair will be hanging over the items in the bag.

Shape the bag and back up to the bottom of the hat.

Shape the back of the hat and the area above the bag.

Begin working on the face by pushing the forehead back.

Continue to shape the hat more deeply.

Round both sides of the beard.

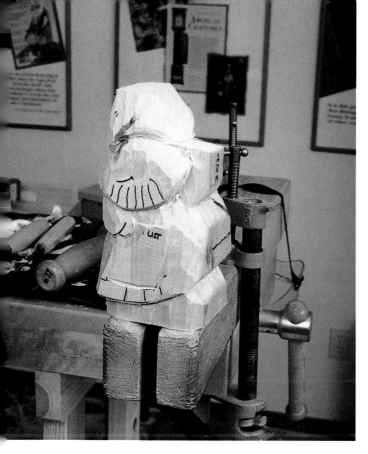

Shape the face area by sloping it back some so that Santa will look as if he is gazing slightly upward.

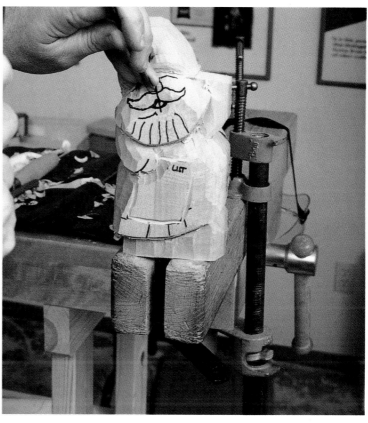

Using a small "U" gouge, put a stop cut under the end of Santa's nose.

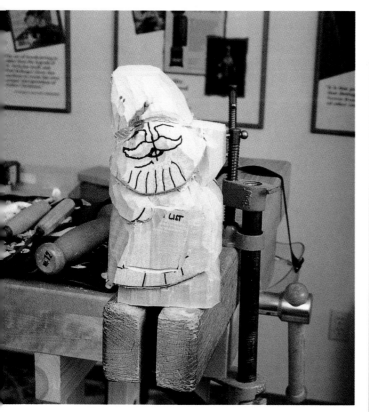

Re-establish the centerline and re-draw the face onto the piece.

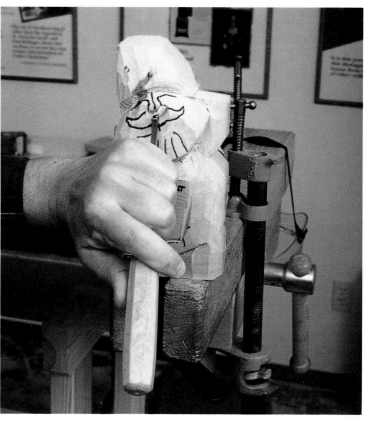

Cut up to the stop cut with a small "U" gouge.

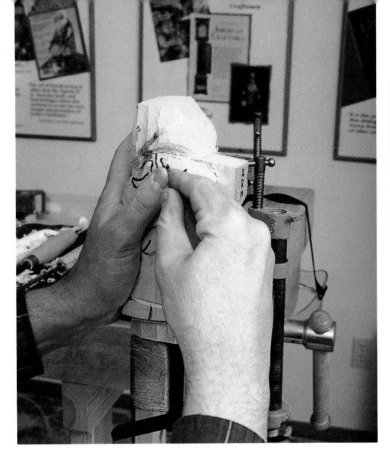

Cut along both sides of Santa's nose with a small "V" gouge or knife.

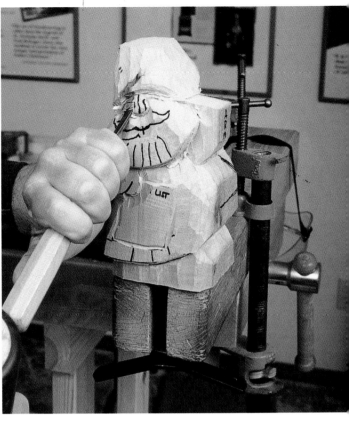

Cut up to the stop cuts above the eyes. Don't remove more than 1/8" or so at this time.

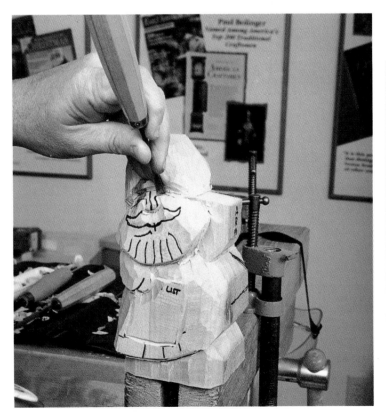

Use a medium "U" gouge to set in a stop cut above each eye.

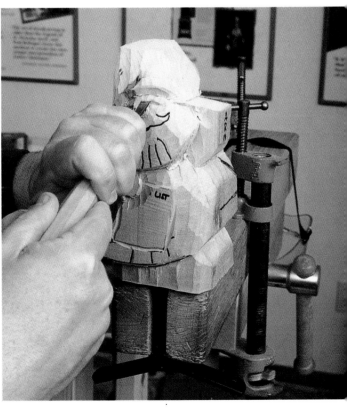

Slope the forehead farther back and then re-cut the eyes deeper this time.

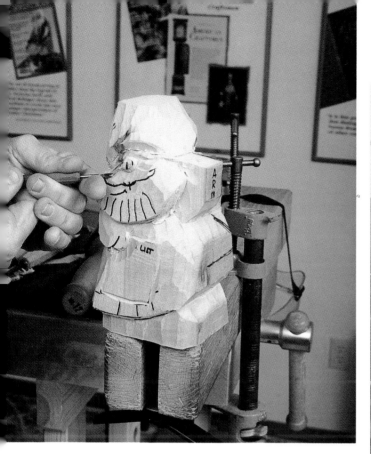

Cut the top of the mustache and slope the mustache itself back toward the bottom of the nose and the cheeks.

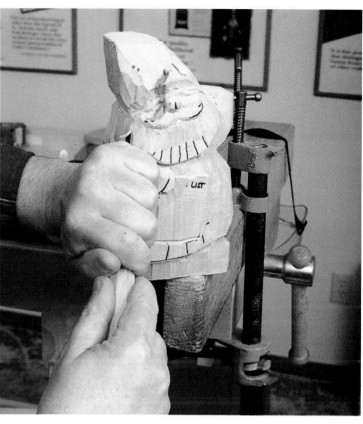

Shape the beard up to the bottom of the mustache.

Make stop cuts along the bottom of the mustache and remove the excess wood from below the mustache.

Cut the bottom of the hat farther back.

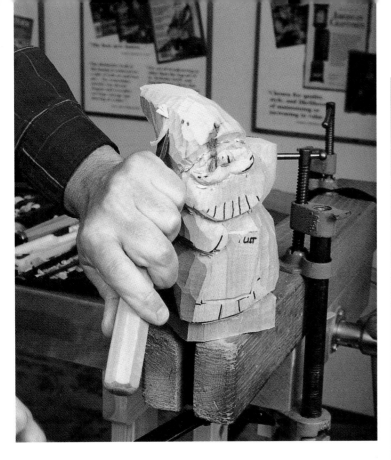

Shape the side of the hat slightly.

After making a groove and a stop cut all the way around the tassel, use a "U" gouge to remove the wood below the tassel.

When the hat is shaped the way you want it, draw lines as shown to mark the areas for cuts to define the tassel and the fur trim.

Shape the tassel all the way around the hat.

Cut a groove all the way around the hat on the lower line to define the top of the fur trim. Use a "U" gouge to remove the wood above the groove to shape the hat.

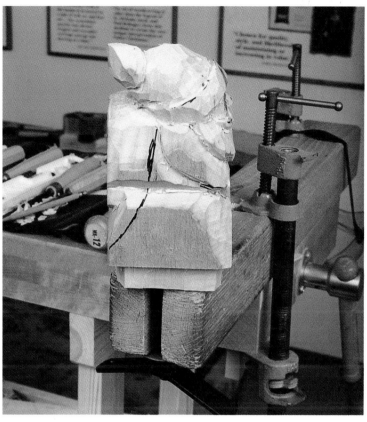

Mark the line that shows the slope of the lower coat and the side of Santa's bag.

Mark the mitten and coat sleeve, then cut the mitten down away from the coat sleeve.

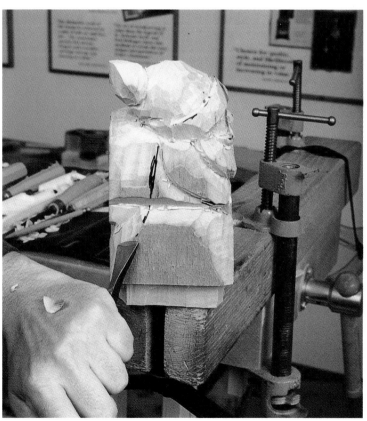

Shape the coat.

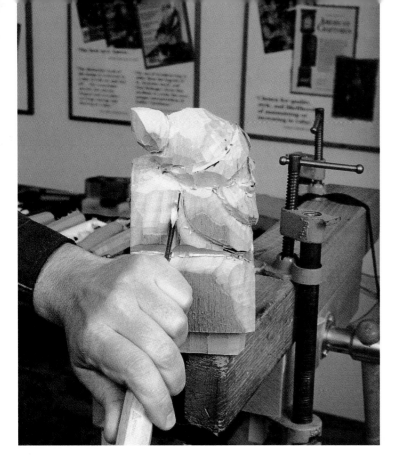

Cut along the line on the bag with a "V" gouge, then shape the bag with a "U" gouge.

At this point the basic Santa is carved. Now redraw the lines showing the details on all sides.

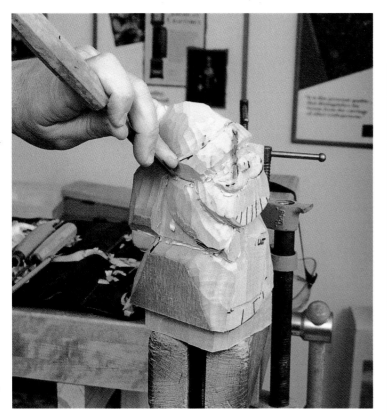

Deepen the stop cut at the bottom of the hat and round the shoulder and bag into the deepened cut.

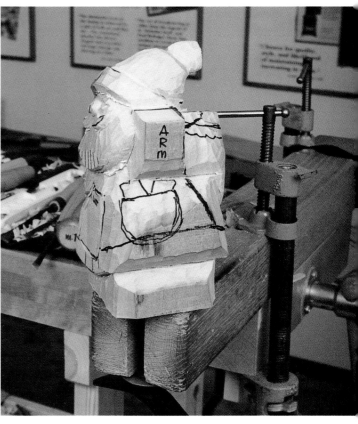

The left-side with the pocket and details drawn on.

Back view with items drawn poking out of the bag. From right to left these items are a candy cane, a teddy bear, and some chocolate bars.

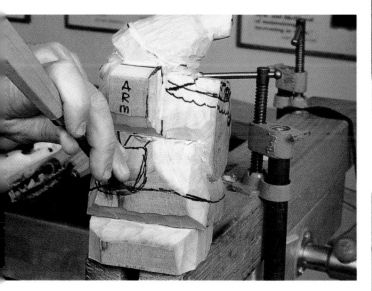

Make a stop cut around the pocket and remove the wood below. Don't go too deep — remember this is only a pocket.

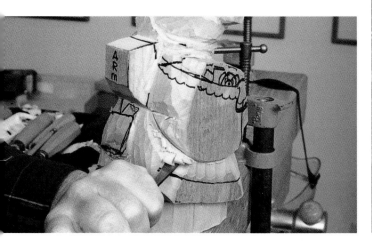

Cut away the excess wood from behind the pocket. Make a stop cut along the side and base of the bag and remove the excess wood below the side of the bag.

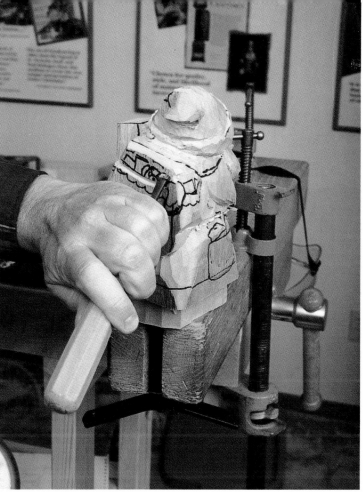

Cut a groove at the top of the bag. Begin cutting away to leave the details sticking out of the bag.

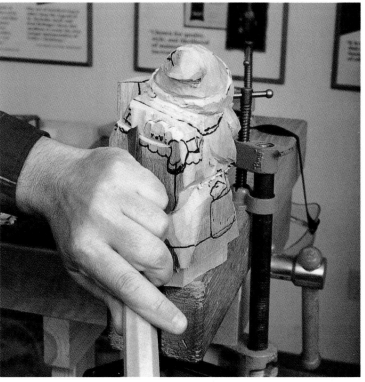

Cut details into the wood above the bag. Don't go past the line drawn where Santa's hair will come.

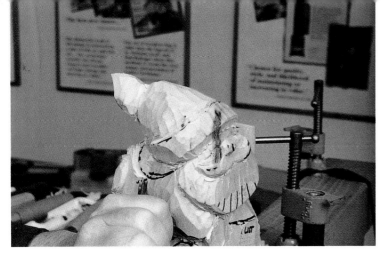

Use a "V" gouge to cut a groove along the hairline.

Finish trimming up the details sticking out of the bag. Cut them all the way in to where they meet the hair line.

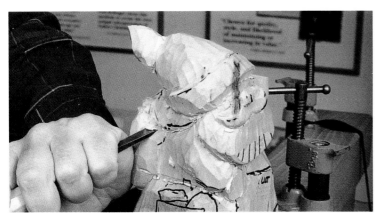

Cut away excess wood to reveal the hair line.

Cut the hair and hat definition a little deeper to show off the hat a little more.

Make stop cuts along the bottom of the bag decoration. Remove wood from below the stop cut to define the bag decoration.

Make stop cuts around the right pocket and the items sticking out of it. Remove the wood below and around the pocket.

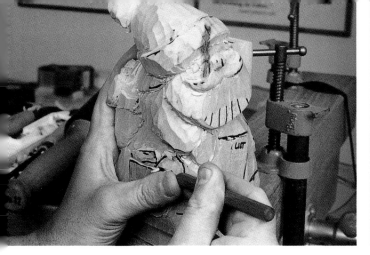

Cut along the top of the pocket to separate it from the details. Carve the details sticking out of the pocket.

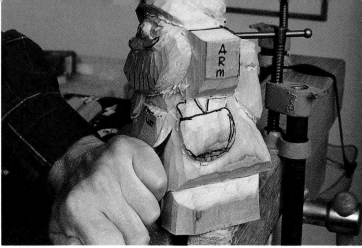

Shape all around the front, sides, and back one more time. If you need, to you may add depth anywhere by cutting stop cuts and removing wood to make details more visible.

Shape the coat below, behind, and in front of the pocket and objects sticking out of the pocket.

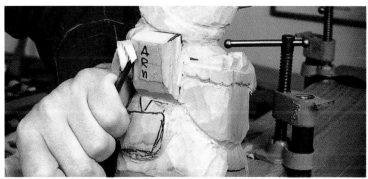

Shape the arm and round it on three sides.

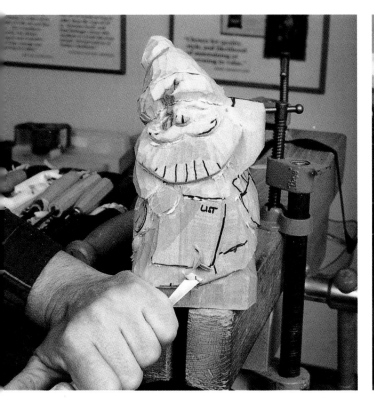

Shape Santa's list up to the mitten and remove wood around the list to help define it.

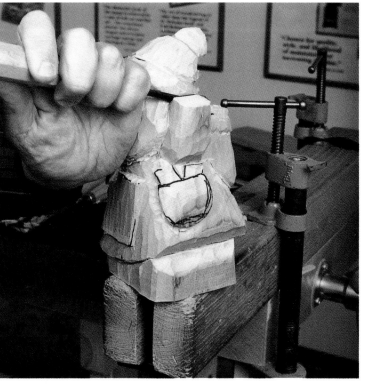

Cut the wood from between the arm and Santa's hat.

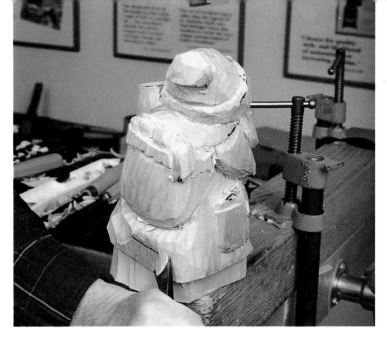

Finish cleaning up the coat bottom.

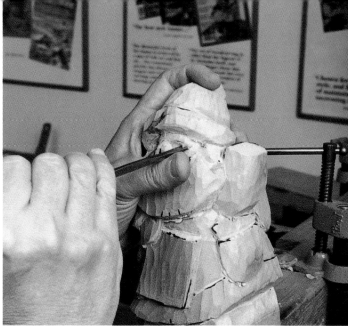

Recut the eyes, nose, and mustache to deepen them.

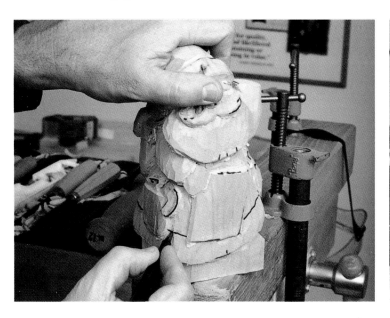

Draw a line for the top of the fur all the way around the coat.

Draw the lower lip in place. Make a stop cut under the lip and remove the wood from under the lip. Be careful here — just a little.

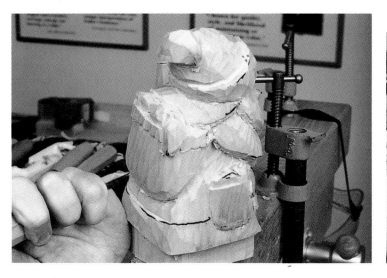

Cut a groove all the way around the coat on the fur line.

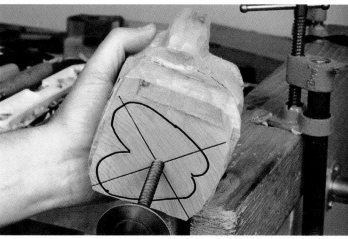

Draw the outline of the bottom of Santa's boots.

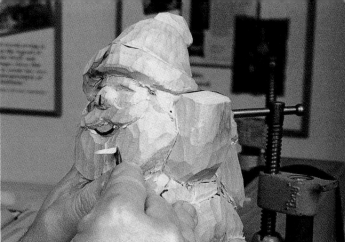

Make stop cuts with a firmer all the way around the bottom of the coat. Remove excess wood. Repeat until you have cut the bottom of the boots back to the drawn line.

Use a small "V" gouge to cut the hairs into Santa's beard. Be as tame or as wild as you like.

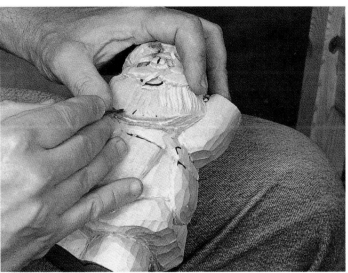

Shape the top of the boot from the front up to the bottom of the coat. Shape the rest of the boots as you like.

At this point, the Santa is ready for the details to be cut in. Note: The pattern showed a hand atop the upright arm. I decided along the way to leave the arm full length and to add a hand later. You may cut the hand there now or wait and add one as I did.

I removed the carving from the carver's arm to get a better cutting angle.

Use a small "V" gouge to put grooves into Santa's hair.

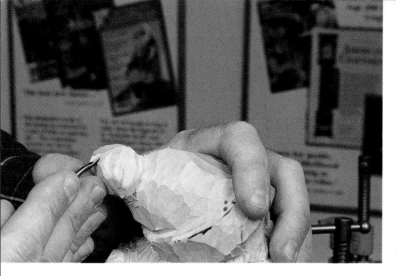

Use a small "V" gouge to put marks onto the tassel to indicate fur trim.

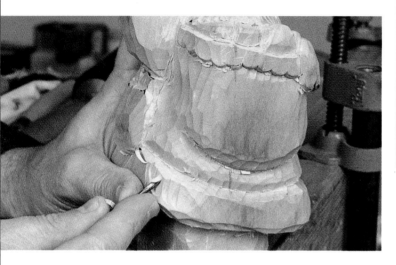

Use a small "V" gouge to put texture onto the fur trim at the bottom of Santa's coat.

Use a small "V" gouge to cut across Santa's bag to show some texture on the bag. Note: At this point I use a Foredom tool with diamond tips to sand all the crevice and clean up the piece for painting. The figure is then hand sanded with 120, 240, and 400 grit papers to fully prepare it for painting. Sand lightly to leave tool marks but enough to get rid of things that will catch up in the brush.

Front/right view of the sanded figure. The figure has been base coated with an off-white sealer.

Front/left view of the figure ready for painting.

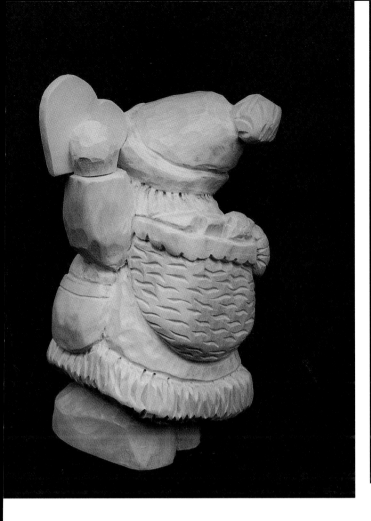

Back/left view of the figure ready for painting.

Back/right view of the figure ready for painting.

The hat, beard, and some other areas like the fur trim are painted white first. When the white is dry spray with two light coats of Tuffilm matte spray (or a similar protective spray of your preference). Afterward, Cardinal Red is applied to the hat and coat areas. All painting is done with acrylic paint for these figures. We use Tuffilm matte spray during and after the painting. The final coat of Tuffilm matte gives a slight sheen to the work.

Large areas are painted quickly without regard to "cutting in." Later the figure will be sprayed again and these areas will be "cut in" since this seems to make the painting a smoother process.

Another view of the painting.

Butter Yellow is used as the color for Santa's bag.

Medium Flesh, with a drop or two of Cardinal Red mixed in, is used for Santa's face.

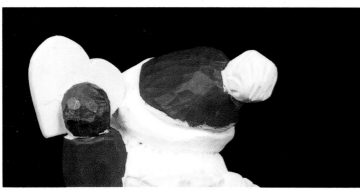

Christmas Green is used for the mittens.

Brown (chocolate) was used for the candy heart and some of the candy bars.

46

Cloudberry is used for Teddy and dark brown for one chocolate bar.

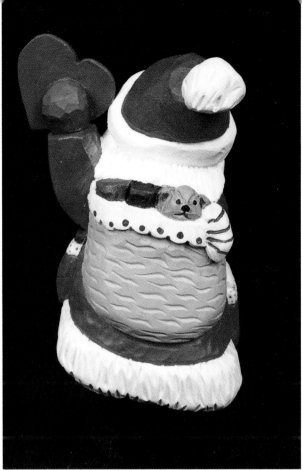

More details.

Some details are added to show the candy canes and the pocket fur.

The chocolate heart is lettered in white. Santa's list is lettered in black. To detail Santa's eyes, a white stripe is painted first. Light blue is put over the white, leaving a little white showing. A black pupil is added. Finally, a white dot is added on the pupils to create some sparkle.

Chapter Five
The Photo Gallery

In this gallery you will find front and back or front and side shots of many designs I have done. Some are retired, some are in production, and some are new designs. This section is intended as the "idea" section where you can let your mind wander and daydream about your own designs. Have fun.

Here are the patterns for the chocoholic Santa and five others shown in this book. The chocoholic Santa was done on 4" X 4" basswood while the others were done on 2" X 4" basswood. You will not need side views of the ones made from 2" X 4" wood since the sides will come naturally to you after you have carved some of the front and back. Sizes for figures are shown along with their pictures.

Santa has a golf bag full of other candy cane clubs.

This piece shows a disheartened Santa leaning against a skinny, crooked chimney. This figure is approximately 9" tall.

This is Santa as a fantasy golfer. He is using a candy cane club to hit a snowball. This piece was popular, in great part, because of the popularity of golf. This figure is approximately 8" tall.

"You are what you eat" is true even from the back I guess.

On the back side we see that Santa's bag is way too big to fit down the skinny little chimney. The piece is titled "Mission Impossible" which says it all. By the way, this piece is also a candle holder — the candle fits down into the chimney.

I have often been told "you are what you eat" and it is certainly true in the case of this Santa. He has obviously had so many cookies that he is turning into one. This figure is approximately 81/2" tall.

This piece is titled "Wishful Thinking." Here Santa has come down the chimney and discovered a huge stocking awaiting him. Do you remember when you were a kid you thought the bigger the stocking the more you would get? This figure is approximately 9" tall.

On the back of "Wishful Thinking" you can see that Santa's basket is too small to be used to fill the huge stocking he found.

Back view of Santa the golfer.

While not strictly a Santa, this golfing angel is still humorous. Even his golf ball has wings ... and I happen to know that he can hit that ball over 12,000 yards! The title is "Yes They Play Golf in Heaven." This figure is approximately 8" tall.

"Santa's Day Off" is probably not as humorous as many designs but it is amusing none-the-less to think of Santa as a golf buff. Do you think he shaves strokes from his score? This figure is approximately 9" tall.

Back view.

Back view of "Been There Done That."

This little guy is an elf and not a true Santa but he is still humorous and worth a look. He also sells well. By the way, did you know that the best way to save the reindeer is in the freezer with the other meat? This figure is approximately 9 1/2" tall.

This is one of my best selling designs even though there was some worry that the message might be too negative. The written message carries the piece but I think he is cute with his little gut and his little butt hanging out. This figure is approximately 8" tall.

Back view of "Save the Reindeer."

He's even funny from the back.

This is a new design that should be selling well since it has all the elements of design and a very funny subject if you remember the 1992 presidential campaign. This figure is approximately 7" tall.

This is one version of the "On Strike for More Cookies" design that lost out over the final version. I still find it appealing. This figure is approximately 6" tall.

Back view.

Back view of "Diet."

This little guy has a spoon in one hand and a banana split in the other. This figure is approximately 5" tall.

This is an early design titled "Surprise." The surprise is that he is doing nothing until you turn him around. This figure is approximately 7" tall.

When you see his back, you see that his bag is torn and the toys are falling out. It doesn't matter though since this is a magic bag and no matter what falls out — your toys are still in there. This piece did O.K. but it needed too much explanation to be a hit. It lacked the elements of action and detail. With this carving I learned not to put the hook on the back of a carving.

This view shows Santa is reading a book that will help with his annual trip around the world.

This piece is called "Claus-a-lounger" and shows Santa sitting in the special chair the elves made for him because he is such a good boss. This figure is approximately 7" X 7" X 4".

This is a 1998 design showing Santa on the slopes with his Tundra Runners, ski pass, and very fancy boots. This figure is approximately 7 1/2" tall.

SKI CLAUS

2"x 4" BASSWOOD

Back view of Ski Santa.

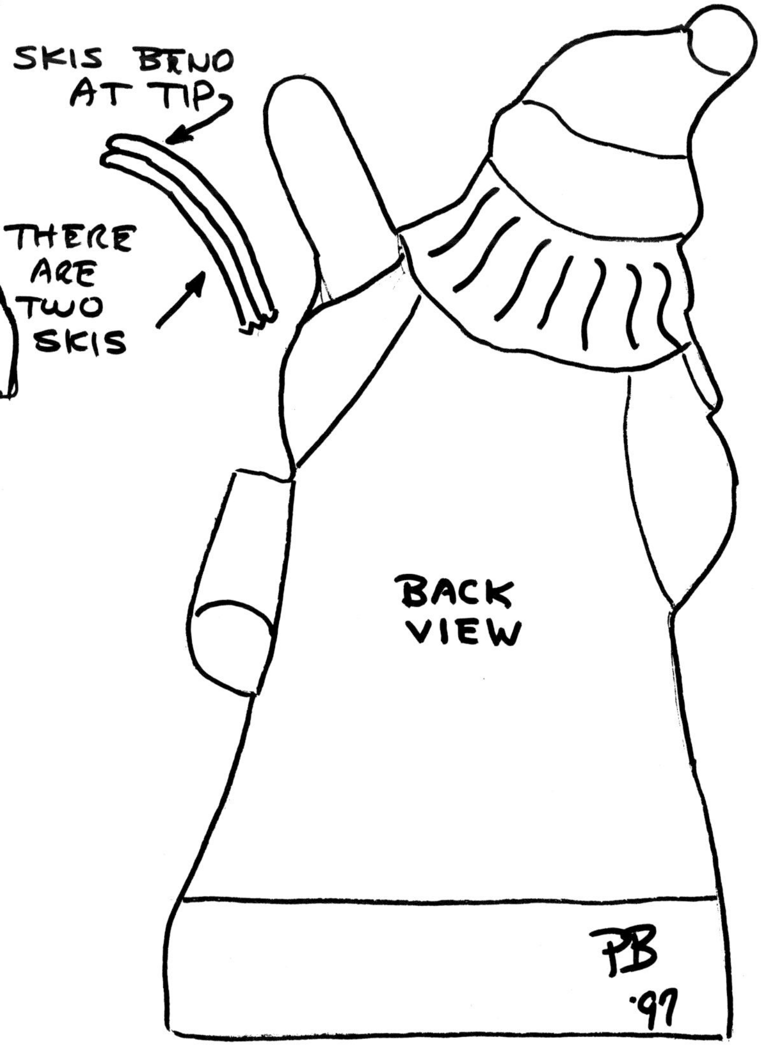

TUNDRA RUNNERS

SKI PASS

SKIS BEND AT TIP

THERE ARE TWO SKIS

PB '97

BACK VIEW

PB '97

Enlarge 135% for original size.

CAT LOVER CLAUS

2"x 4" BASSWOOD

DRAWN
ACTUAL
SIZE

CAT LOVER CLAUS

DRAWN
ACTUAL
SIZE

BACK
VIEW

PB
'97

This Santa is trying to keep the cat nip away
from his furry friends. He probably got the stuff
as a Christmas present for them but didn't get a
chance to hide it. This figure is approximately 8"
tall.

Back view of the
cat nip Santa.

CHOO CHOO CLAUS

2" x 4" BASSWOOD

CARVE OR
PAINT YOUR
OWN DETAILS.

DRAWN
ACTUAL
SIZE

NOTE: TRAIN
GOES AROUND
SIDE OF
SANTA.

PB
'97

CHOO CHOO CLAUS

PB '97

CARVE OR
PAINT YOUR
OWN
DETAILS

The train goes on around his side. The details on the train help make the piece appealing. The piece isn't really humorous but it is appealing.

Here Santa is a model railroad buff with his train and his North Pole Railroad cap. This figure is approximately 7 1/2" tall.

2"X4" BASSWOOD

PSYCHIC
SANTA
"HE KNOWS"

DRAWN
ACTUAL SIZE

NORTH POLE
PSYCHIC HOTLINE

PB '97

PSYCHIC SANTA

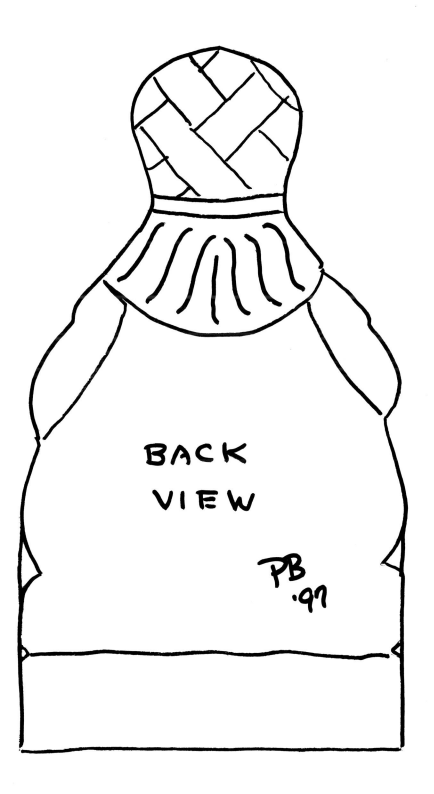

BACK
VIEW

PB
.97

PSYCHIC SANTA
PREDICTIONS

The Psychic Santa knows if you've been good or bad but he also predicts — this time he's calling for peace on earth. This figure is approximately 7 1/2" tall.

Back view of Psychic Santa.

"LEPRACLAUS"
GOOD LUCK SANTA

DRAWN ACTUAL SIZE

CARVE OR PAINT YOUR OWN DETAILS

GOLD

DB '97

"LEPRA CLAUS"
GOOD LUCK SANTA

This leprechaun Santa has a bag of gold and a shamrock to show us. This figure is approximately 6" tall.

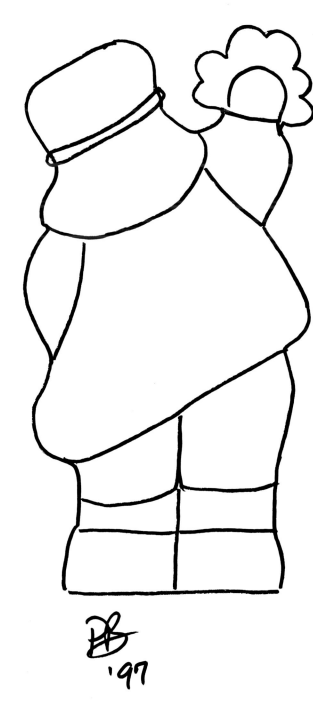

This is a very simple back that helps keep pricing down in the reproductions.

This is the tool Santa. He has his hard hat, hammer, tool box, and power tools. So, do you think he's a union member? This figure is approximately 7" tall.

This tiny JOY Santa has a humorous posture. This figure is approximately 5 1/2" tall.

More stuff on Santa's reverse view.

The other side.